UNNATURAL DISASTERS

LETHAL LEAKS AND SPILLS

By Danielle Haynes

Gareth Stevens
PUBLISHING

Please visit our website, www.garethstevens.com. For a free color catalog of all our high-quality books, call toll free 1-800-542-2595 or fax 1-877-542-2596.

Library of Congress Cataloging-in-Publication Data

Names: Haynes, Danielle, author.
Title: Lethal leaks and spills / Danielle Haynes.
Description: New York : Gareth Stevens Publishing, [2018] | Series: Unnatural disasters | Includes bibliographical references and index.
Identifiers: LCCN 2017001082| ISBN 9781538204405 (pbk. book) | ISBN 9781538204412 (6 pack) | ISBN 9781538204429 (library bound book)
Subjects: LCSH: Chemical spills–Juvenile literature.
Classification: LCC TD196.C45 H377 2018 | DDC 363.17–dc23
LC record available at https://lccn.loc.gov/2017001082

First Edition

Published in 2018 by
Gareth Stevens Publishing
111 East 14th Street, Suite 349
New York, NY 10003

Designer: Sam DeMartin
Editor: Joan Stoltman

Photo credits: Cover, p. 1 jukurae/Shutterstock.com; p. 5 (image 1) jupiter8/ Shutterstock.com; p. 5 (image 2) MNI/Shutterstock.com; p. 5 (image 3) Igor Kovalchuk/ Shutterstock.com; p. 5 (image 4) SOMMAI/Shutterstock.com; p. 5 (image 5) DPS/ Shutterstock.com; p. 7 (top) MCT/Tribune News Service/Getty Images; p. 7 (bottom) Belovodchenko Anton/Shutterstock.com; p. 9 DOMINIQUE FAGET/AFP/Getty Images; pp. 11, 13 (both) arindambanerjee/Shutterstock.com; p. 15 (map) Peter Hermes Furian/ Shutterstock.com; p. 15 (top) Victor Rotaru/Shutterstock.com; p. 17 (top) Chris Hondros/ Hulton Archive/Getty Images; p. 17 (bottom) Bloomberg/Bloomberg/Getty Images; p. 18 Keystone-France/Gamma-Keystone/Getty Images; p. 19 Laurent MAOUS/Gamma-Rapho/Getty Images; p. 21 (both) CHRIS WILKINS/AFP/Getty Images; p. 23 (top) Miami Herald/Tribune News Service/Getty Images; p. 23 (bottom) U.S. Coast Guard/Getty Images News/Getty Images; p. 24 Bettmann/Bettmann/Getty Images; p. 25 Joe Raedle/Getty Images News/Getty Images; p. 26 Historical/Corbis Historical/Getty Images; p. 27 frees/Shutterstock.com; p. 29 (bottom) Brent Olson/ Shutterstock.com; p. 29 (top) Jim Barber/Shutterstock.com.

Printed in China

CPSIA compliance information: Batch #CS17GS: For further information contact Gareth Stevens, New York, New York at 1-800-542-2595.

CONTENTS

Words in the glossary appear in **bold** type
the first time they are used in the text.

ACCIDENTS THAT HURT ECOSYSTEMS

Spilling soda on the floor is no big deal—you just grab a towel and wipe it up. But toxic chemicals spilled into the ocean, leaked into the air, or dumped onto land can't just be wiped away. Chemicals are often so hard to get out of the **environment** once they're spilled that cleanups can last for years. And chemical leaks and spills often affect the health and homes of people and animals in the area immediately!

The deadly impact on an ecosystem can, sadly, last even beyond a cleanup of an area. The ecosystem's balance is upset as parts of the food chain are harmed or killed by leaks and spills. These accidents have been happening for decades—and continue to happen today!

POISON IN FOOD CHAINS

Some leaks and spills put poisons into the environment that don't kill quickly. Heavy metals stay inside an animal or person who's been exposed for a long time, poisoning them slowly. Heavy metals are used a lot in manufacturing to make batteries, electronics, and more. For years, these factories sat along waterways and dumped their wastewater into them. This exposed local fish to heavy metals. The poisonous metals then transferred to everyone who ate the fish!

FOOD CHAIN POISONING

1. A chemical spill happens near a body of water.

2. Algae take in the poisoned water.

3. A small fish eats the now-poisoned algae.

5. The poison then travels to whoever eats the bigger fish—a shark, a bear, or even a human!

4. A larger fish eats the smaller fish, and it's now poisoned as well.

LASTING EFFECT

Heavy metals occur naturally in the environment, but cause **cancer** and other serious health problems in animals and humans. They include lead, mercury, arsenic, copper, zinc, silver, and many more.

TOXIC MUD SPILL IN TENNESSEE

In 2008, the dirt wall of a man-made "pond" broke at a coal-burning power plant in Tennessee. Thick, toxic coal waste poured over land, into rivers, and through homes. The deadly mud—called coal ash—is made of water and ash left over from burning coal. It contains several poisons, including arsenic, mercury, and lead.

☢ LASTING EFFECT

In 2015, the Environmental Protection Agency (EPA) said how coal ash should be handled, but didn't call it hazardous, or dangerous. This was good news for the coal industries, but bad news to environmentalists!

For years, **environmentalists** have complained that storing coal ash in these "ponds" poisons groundwater, thus poisoning water supplies. But who could have imagined one of the worst environmental **disasters** in American history? The company that owned the plant didn't even know how much coal ash they were storing. It estimated half as much as scientists later determined was actually spilled.

Those gray mountains in the center of a rural landfill in Alabama are coal ash that was transported there from the spill cleanup in Tennessee.

TENNESSEE COAL ASH SPILL FAST FACTS

- **what:** 1.1 billion gallons (4.2 billion L) of coal ash, a decade's worth of waste from burning coal, spilled

- **where:** Roane County, Tennessee

- **when:** December 22, 2008

- **immediate effects:** three houses totally destroyed and dozens more damaged; roads and rails blocked; 300 acres (121 ha) of land covered with it; trees snapped out of the ground

- **long-term effects:** billions of dollars and a cleanup that will take decades; damaged ecosystems; poisoned water supplies

7

WASTEWATER SPILL IN SPAIN

In 1998, one of the worst environmental disasters in European history threatened Doñana National Park, Spain's largest nature reserve. An industrial dam burst at a nearby zinc and silver mine. Toxins being stored in a man-made pond with dirt walls spilled out in **sludge** made up of mining waste. The muddy material—filled with many harmful heavy metals—headed right for the park!

AZNALCÓLLAR WASTEWATER SPILL FAST FACTS

- **what:** 1.3 million gallons (4.9 million L) of mining wastewater spilled

- **where:** Aznalcóllar, Spain

- **when:** April 25, 1998

- **short-term effects:** 22,000 people had no clean water; wells, marshes, floodplains, and rivers poisoned; 2,000 birds and 41 tons (37 mt) of fish harmed; 8,649 acres (3,500 ha) of crops destroyed

- **long-term effects:** 25,000 acres (10,000 ha) of farmland plus all nearby groundwater and wetlands damaged for decades; diseases and cancers appeared in animals years later

An emergency dam was built to protect the park, an international treasure and home to over 250 bird species. The dam stopped the sludge from getting into the park, but it didn't

stop the toxins from entering the park's delicate ecosystem. Animals in the local food web brought the heavy metals into the park, as did **contaminated** groundwater that connected to the park's swamps and water supply.

Many thousands of fish were killed after the mud spilled into rivers. Nets were pulled through the water to collect the floating, dead bodies off the surface.

GAS LEAK IN INDIA

In 1984, thousands of people in Bhopal, India, died or were sickened by a toxic gas they could smell, but not see. After an explosion at a chemical plant, a poisonous gas called methyl isocyanate (eye-soh-SY-uh-nayt) was released from a holding tank, poisoning several nearby neighborhoods. Those who didn't die suffered breathing problems and blindness and later developed illnesses such as lung cancer.

Thirty years after the disaster, the effects are still everywhere to see. Toxic-waste exposure and contaminated drinking water continue to this day. Over 120,000 people still regularly seek treatment for health problems related to gas exposure. Decades after the explosion, children have been born deformed or suffering serious health problems. And still the 70-acre (28 ha) site has no healthcare services or cleanup effort.

ANOTHER MINING DISASTER

On October 21, 1966, at 9:15 a.m., thousands of tons of coal-mining waste stored at the top of a mountain poured over Aberfan, Wales. Witnesses say they could hear the landslide as it came down the mountain toward the village like a roar. The disaster killed 144 people. At Pantglas Junior School, 116 students were killed, which was half of the student body. It took a week to find all the bodies.

☢ LASTING EFFECT

As much as 27,500 tons (25,000 mt) of contaminated topsoil, 375 tons (340 mt) of toxic raw materials, and several square miles of poisoned groundwater still need to be cleaned.

This slum, or poor neighborhood, built near the plant that exploded in Bhopal has no clean water source, so residents have to use contaminated water to cook, drink, clean, and bathe.

Bhopal is considered the world's worst industrial accident. But who's to blame? Residents blame the plant's American owners for the explosion and for not cleaning up after it. They sued the company, which agreed to pay the victims roughly $550 per person, hardly enough to cover continuing medical costs and funeral costs or to repay for the death of a loved one.

A former plant engineer claims many corners were cut to save money in the building, maintenance, training, and safety measures of the plant. Others claimed that a worker caused the gas leak on purpose. Whatever the cause, the Bhopal disaster scared many countries into passing industry safety laws. But few changes have happened in India, so protests continue regularly in Bhopal to this day.

BHOPAL LEAK FAST FACTS

- **what:** 45 tons (41 mt) of toxic methyl isocyanate gas leaked

- **where:** Bhopal, India

- **when:** December 2 and 3, 1984

- **short-term effects:** 570,000 people exposed; half of the existing pregnancies immediately failed; thousands died within days (some say as many as 30,000); animals killed

- **long-term effects:** 20,000 more have died and 555,000 sickened in the following decades, many of whom weren't even alive in 1984

LASTING EFFECT

No one at Union Carbide, the company that owned the plant, and no one who worked at the plant ever served jail time for the Bhopal disaster.

There's still no cleanup effort or help for the victims' many medical needs. Decades later, many locals still show up to protest on the anniversary of the disaster.

TOXIC MINING IN
ROMANIA

Gold may be one of the most valuable metals in the world, but the process of mining it from the ground has toxic results. Many gold mining companies use cyanide, a natural poison, in a chemical process to remove small bits of gold from rock.

In 2000, a dam in Baia Mare, Romania, that held back a pool of cyanide at a gold mine broke. Millions of gallons of the poison and heavy metals spilled into the Somes, the Tisza, and the Danube Rivers as well as the Black Sea. As the toxic water traveled, government officials closed underwater gates to stop the poison from spreading to other branches of Europe's famous Danube River. Still, the poison reached Hungary and Yugoslavia, killing fish in both countries.

BAIA MARE CYANIDE SPILL FAST FACTS

- **what:** 26.4 million gallons (100 million L) of cyanide-poisoned water spilled

- **where:** Baia Mare, Romania

- **when:** January 30, 2000

- **short-term effects:** ecosystem destroyed; poisoned drinking water for millions in three countries; over 1,240 tons (1,125 mt) of fish died in Hungary alone; foxes, otters, and birds died from eating toxic fish

- **long-term effects:** full river ecosystem recovery will take decades; 20 protected species' habitats were damaged, hurting the species' chances of survival

14

When chemicals spill into a river, like the cyanide in Romania, the toxic substance will travel downstream, possibly polluting other bodies of water and hundreds of miles of land.

UKRAINE

Baia Mare

HUNGARY

MOLDOVA

ROMANIA

Belgrade

Bucharest

BLACK SEA

YUGOSLAVIA

BULGARIA

LASTING EFFECT

Several countries have banned the use of cyanide in gold mining. After the Baia Mare disaster, Romania considered a ban three times but still hasn't passed one.

15

OIL SPILLS: NO SMALL PROBLEM

The Niger River delta continues to be one of the worst environmental disaster sites in the world. Oil companies have been spilling oil there repeatedly since the 1970s with no regard for the damage it's doing to animals, the ecosystem, and even people. Between 1976 and 2001 alone, there were 6,817 oil spills totaling 126 million gallons (477 million L) of oil in just this one part of the world!

The reckless behavior and policies of the oil companies in the area have poisoned soil 16 feet (5 m) deep, as well as groundwater, which poisons local residents' drinking wells. In 2011, scientists tested sites in a region of the delta called Ogoniland, including areas that were supposedly cleaned. Over 4,000 samples proved that even cleaned areas were still highly toxic.

LASTING EFFECT

Scientists decided that Ogoniland needs $1 billion in work and cleanup and will take 30 years to recover. The entire Niger River delta needs cleaning, too, but that may take as much as $100 billion!

Oil has destroyed some of the region's beautiful forests.

NIGER DELTA OIL SPILLS FAST FACTS

- **what:** crude oil, which is unprocessed oil that has over 2,000 chemicals in it, spilled

- **where:** the 27,000-square-mile (70,000 sq km) Niger River delta in Nigeria; especially a 386-square-mile (1,000 sq km) area of Ogoniland

- **when:** 1950s to present; 1950s to 1990s in Ogoniland

- **effects:** dead animals; damage to entire ecosystems; people in the country are exposed to so much toxic pollution that they live less than 50 years on average

...tion. That's what happened in 1978, when a storm
coast of northwestern France caused the Amoco
il **supertanker** to crash into rocks. The ship
nto parts, spilling 68 million gallons (257.4
n L) of crude oil.

he oil reached 240 miles (386 km) along the coast
ce, destroying ecosystems by killing millions
nals. The French navy tried to get to the ship and
e spill, but bad weather and rocky conditions
the tanker
ft pouring
to the ocean
eeks! Less
ne-third
oil was
ered in the
up, though
s no way to
if the rest of
l **dispersed**
yed in
ea.

LASTING EFFECT

In 1988, a judge ordered the owners of the
supertanker to pay France for cleanup
costs, but France wanted much more
than the $85.2 million offered. In 1992,
$200 million was finally agreed on.

In Portsall, France, and many other villages along the coast of France, oil turned the beautiful, sandy beaches black.

AMOCO CADIZ SPILL FAST FACTS

- **what:** 68 million gallons (257.4 million L) of crude oil spilled

- **when:** March 16, 1978

- **where:** Atlantic Ocean off the coast of Portsall, France, and Channel Islands

- **short-term effects:** millions of sea creatures, 20,000 birds, and 9,000 tons (8,164 mt) of oysters killed

- **long-term effects:** ecosystem contamination continued through oil trapped in sediment onshore and oil coating the seafloor

Since March 24, 1989, when the Exxon Valdez oil tanker struck a reef off the southern coast of Alaska, Prince William Sound has never been the same. Millions of gallons of crude oil spilled and soon spread to 1,500 miles (2,414 km) of coastline—about the length of California's coast! It also spread throughout 10,000 square miles (26,000 sq km) of ocean—an area the size of Maryland!

The spill happened inside a sound, which is a long and broad ocean inlet. This means the oil couldn't disperse and affected a small area more strongly than the same amount of oil would if it had been able to spread across more water. Plus, since it took days for the cleanup to start, a lot of damage was done.

EXXON VALDEZ SPILL FAST FACTS

- **what:** 11 million gallons (42 million L) of crude oil spilled

- **where:** Prince William Sound, Alaska

- **when:** March 24, 1989, 12:04 a.m.

- **short-term effects:** 250,000 to 500,000 birds, up to 5,500 sea otters, 300 harbor seals, 22 orcas, and untold numbers of fish died

- **long-term effects:** only 3 to 14 percent of the oil was recovered, so the ecosystem is still poisoned; only 2 of 26 studied species populations recovered; breeding issues, deformities, tumors, and more for many animals

☢ LASTING EFFECT

Because the Exxon Valdez disaster was such a tragedy and so widely known, the Oil Pollution Act passed through Congress very quickly. The 1990 law made oil-transportation industry regulations, or rules, for safety and emergencies more strict.

Photographs of wildlife in the aftermath of the spill made newspapers and magazines across the world. They're still used today by environmentalists because they're so powerful!

Only one other accident dumped more oil in the United States than the *Exxon Valdez* disaster—the explosion of the Deepwater Horizon oil-drilling rig in 2010. For 87 days, crude oil leaked from a hole in a pipe along the ocean floor. That pipe had connected oil beneath the ocean floor to the rig. Oil didn't reach land for 17 days, but when it did, beaches in Louisiana, Mississippi, Florida, Texas, and Alabama were devastated, or destroyed. Over 1,000 square miles (2,590 sq km) of seafloor and 1,300 miles (2,092 km) of shoreline were contaminated.

Multiple attempts were made to stop the spill over nearly 3 months, but failed. Experts finally sealed the hole on September 19, 2010. Yet today, more oil continues to appear in the area.

DEEPWATER HORIZON SPILL FAST FACTS

- **what:** 210 million gallons (795 million L) of crude oil spilled

- **where:** 1 mile (1.6 km) beneath the Gulf of Mexico, 40 miles (64 km) from the Louisiana coast

- **when:** April 20, 2010, 10:00 p.m. to July 15, 2010, 2:22 p.m.

- **short-term effects:** thousands of animals killed; poisoned habitats for seven **endangered species**

- **long-term effects:** only 25 percent of the oil removed at most; fishing and tourism industries devastated in five states

LASTING EFFECT

After the oil killed plants with roots that had been keeping marshland in place, large amounts of land began eroding from the coastline in Louisiana, Alabama, and Mississippi. Loss of land means loss of habitat. Animals weren't just poisoned—many lost their home, too!

This jar holds a crude oil sample collected from the surface of the Gulf of Mexico. It's thick, like a paste!

The underwater oil reservoir that the Deepwater Horizon rig was drilling is known as the Maconda well. Large amounts of oil have been seen during flights over the disaster site since it was sealed. The rig's owners admit that oil from the Maconda well is visible on the water's surface, but claim it's a natural seep that was happening before the explosion.

However, several theories exist about why there's new oil in the area. Some think the spill's seal has broken. Others say the hole was never really sealed and the flow from it was only slowed. The scariest theory of all is that a hole has opened up in the ocean floor, possibly even because of the disaster. If this is the case, the oil pushing through the seabed would only make the hole bigger!

THE IXTOC I OIL SPILL

In 1979, the Ixtoc (ISH-tahk) I rig exploded in water off the coast of Mexico. Crude oil spilled into the water for 290 days. The rig was drilling about 160 feet (49 m) deep when it exploded. About 126 million gallons (477 million L) spilled into the water. Gas bubbled up from the ocean floor and started a fire on the ocean's surface that lasted for months. Thousands of animals were killed. The oil reached all the way to the Texas coast!

The effects of the toxic Deepwater Horizon disaster appear all over the affected environments, from the odies of dead fish piling onshore to marshland changing color as thick, black water flows in from the ocean.

LASTING EFFECT

In 2016, a new set of regulations for offshore oil drilling was announced. Safety requirements and inspections are now stricter, but some say the regulations don't go far enough.

While most oil spills are accidents, the oil disaster that happened in Kuwait in 1991 was done on purpose. The Middle East had erupted in battles over the oil-rich land in Kuwait. Iraq had invaded Kuwait to take over the oil fields, but was soon defeated by US troops. But Iraq didn't surrender quietly. As their troops left Kuwait, they set fire to crude oil wells and lakes and poured million of gallons into the Arabian Gulf to poison the local water supply and environment.

As smoke filled the air, people couldn't breathe, and a toxic rain called acid rain poured over the land. Closer to the fires, it rained oil drops! There was so much black smoke that it blocked the sun and lowered temperatures in some areas.

Some scientists suspect that smoke from the oil fires may have caused permanent climate changes in the Middle East. **Cyclones** that killed over 100,000 people in Bangladesh may have even been one of the long-term effects of this oil disaster!

KUWAITI OIL DISASTER FAST FACTS

- **what:** about 700 oil wells; Kuwait's oil fields; 462 million gallons (1.7 billion L) of crude oil spilled

- **where:** Kuwait

- **when:** January 1991

- **short-term effects:** thousands of birds died; fires burned and smoked for 9 months

- **long-term effects:** 800 miles (1,287 km) of Kuwait and Saudi Arabia coastline poisoned; endangered animals' habitats destroyed; animals sickened; over 400 tons (363 mt) of fish died by 1999; soil contaminated; groundwater poisoned; **ozone layer** damaged; lung cancer and birth deformities caused

Iraq

Iran

Kuwait

Persian Gulf

Saudi Arabia

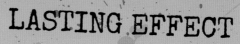

LASTING EFFECT

Over 110,000 US troops returned home from the Middle East with strange symptoms. No one is really sure why they're sick. Many believe oil fumes and chemical and smoke exposure caused their illness, called Gulf War Syndrome.

27

CAN ANYTHING BE DONE?

We live in a world that uses many chemicals, relying on things like oil for our cars and to make plastic. But these practices come at a steep price: Disasters can so easily happen at so many stages of production. Whether it's mining, manufacturing, processing, or transporting, accidents can happen.

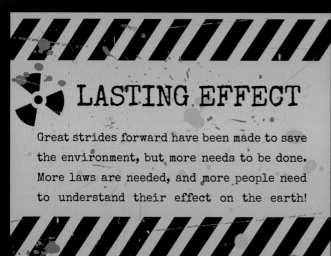

☢ LASTING EFFECT

Great strides forward have been made to save the environment, but more needs to be done. More laws are needed, and more people need to understand their effect on the earth!

But you can help change that! If people used less oil, less would be shipped and drilled for. You and your family can use less fuel by using gas cars less often; taking the bus, subway, or train; walking; or riding your bike. Oil is used to make plastics, so recycling and reusing things made of plastic can make a big difference. Skip using plastic bags at the grocery store, and take your own reusable ones.

Oil, which is commonly measured by the barrel, is mostly used to make fuel for cars, but it's also used to make common products such as footballs, paint, and electronics.

PIPELINE PROTESTS

In recent years, environmentalists have been active in protesting the construction of oil pipelines in the Unites States. Pipelines are built over thousands of miles to transport oil. Pipelines are an environmental issue because they can break and cause disaster. The Keystone XL Pipeline, a 1,179-mile (1,897 km) system that would run from Canada to Nebraska, has been heavily protested. Many protested the Dakota Access Pipeline, a 1,172-mile (1,886 km) system that would run from North Dakota to Illinois, too.

GLOSSARY

cancer: a disease caused by the uncontrolled growth of cells in the body

contaminate: to make unfit for use

cyclone: a powerful storm that forms over water and causes heavy rainfall and high winds

disaster: an event that causes much suffering or loss

disperse: to go or move in different directions; to spread apart

endangered species: a kind of animal that is in danger of dying out

environment: the conditions that surround a living thing and affect the way it lives

environmentalist: a person who works to protect the environment

ozone layer: a layer in the upper atmosphere that prevents dangerous energy from the sun, called radiation, from reaching the surface of Earth

reservoir: a place where something is stored

sludge: a soft, thick, wet material that is produced in various industrial processes

supertanker: a very large ship that has tanks for carrying large amounts of liquid

FOR MORE INFORMATION

BOOKS

Dils, Tracey E. *Oil Spill Cleaner.* Tarrytown, NY: Marshall Cavendish Benchmark, 2011.

Jakubiak, David J. *What Can We Do About Oil Spills and Ocean Pollution?* New York, NY: PowerKids Press, 2012.

Wang, Andrea. *The Science of an Oil Spill.* Ann Arbor, MI: Cherry Lake Publishing, 2015.

Websites

How Oil Affects Birds
bird-rescue.org/our-work/research-and-education/how-oil-affects-birds.aspx
Read all about how birds are helped after an oil spill.

Ranger Rick on the Big Oil Spill
nwf.org/kids/ranger-rick/ranger-rick-on-the-big-oil-spill.aspx
Learn about the Deepwater Horizon spill, and what you can do to help.

What Is an Ecosystem?
eschooltoday.com/ecosystems/what-is-an-ecosystem.html
Read more about ecosystems and how they can be damaged.

INDEX